Most Successful Art Forgers

Bonnie Sheppard

Series Editor
Jeffrey D. Wilhelm

Much thought, debate, and research went into choosing and ranking the 10 items in each book in this series. We realize that everyone has his or her own opinion of what is most significant, revolutionary, amazing, deadly, and so on. As you read, you may agree with our choices, or you may be surprised — and that's the way it should be!

Franklin Watts®
an imprint of
■SCHOLASTIC

www.scholastic.com/librarypublishing

A Rubicon book published in association with Scholastic Inc.

Ru'bïcon © 2007 Rubicon Publishing Inc.
www.rubiconpublishing.com

Associate Publishers: Kim Koh, Miriam Bardswich
Project Editor: Amy Land
Editor: Christine Boocock
Creative Director: Jennifer Drew
Project Manager/Designer: Jeanette MacLean
Graphic Designer: Brandon Köpke

The publisher gratefully acknowledges the following for permission to reprint copyrighted material in this book.

Every reasonable effort has been made to trace the owners of copyrighted material and to make due acknowledgment. Any errors or omissions drawn to our attention will be gladly rectified in future editions.

Cover image: Forged Degas *Dancer on the Stage*, courtesy Karl Sim

"Under the Hammer" from "The Faker's Moll" by Matthew Sweet. *Independent*, January 31, 1999. Reproduced with permission.

"Master Faker," excerpt from pages 171 and 172, *The Art Forger's Handbook* by Eric Hebborn. The Overlook Press. Reproduced with permission.

Library and Archives Canada Cataloguing in Publication

Sheppard, Bonnie
    The 10 most successful art forgers/Bonnie Sheppard.

Includes index.
ISBN 978-1-55448-473-7

    1. Readers (Elementary) 2. Readers—Art forgers. I. Title.
II. Title: Ten most successful art forgers.

PE1117.S47 2007   428.6   C2007-900540-3

1 2 3 4 5 6 7 8 9 10   10   16 15 14 13 12 11 10 09 08 07

Printed in Singapore

Contents

10

18

38

MASTERS OF DECEPTION

What does the term "art expert" mean to you? Maybe this makes you think of someone sitting in a museum, carefully studying dusty old paintings. You might imagine these experts flipping through art history manuals, or inspecting every inch of valuable paintings. The term art expert makes us think of people with the knowledge needed to identify authentic works of art.

But, there are other experts in the art world too. Art forgers are experts who work on the wrong side of the law. In this book, we investigated the most expert art forgers. The ones we ranked the highest completely mastered the styles and techniques of famous artists. They fooled the largest number of museums and critics with their fakes. Some had an influence on the art world and the way paintings are examined. The art forgers who made the most money were also highly ranked. Other forgers on our list specialized in creating provenances, or histories, for fake paintings. Their fake documents often meant more to experts than the paintings themselves.

Every story is unique and every forger gives an exciting glimpse into the criminal world of art forging! As you read, ask yourself:

provenances: *documents that prove the origin and past ownership of works of art*

What does it take to be
THE MOST SUCCESSFUL ART FORGER?

10 OTTO WACKER

Otto Wacker (left) on trial in 1932 with his forged van Gogh paintings in the background

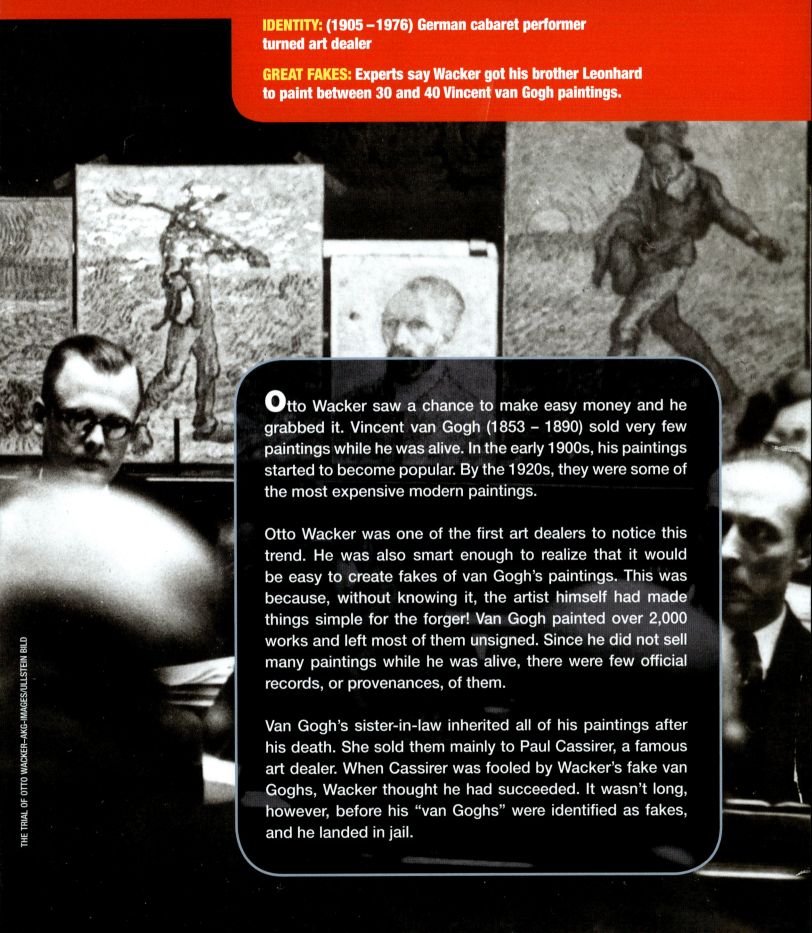

IDENTITY: (1905 –1976) German cabaret performer turned art dealer

GREAT FAKES: Experts say Wacker got his brother Leonhard to paint between 30 and 40 Vincent van Gogh paintings.

Otto Wacker saw a chance to make easy money and he grabbed it. Vincent van Gogh (1853 – 1890) sold very few paintings while he was alive. In the early 1900s, his paintings started to become popular. By the 1920s, they were some of the most expensive modern paintings.

Otto Wacker was one of the first art dealers to notice this trend. He was also smart enough to realize that it would be easy to create fakes of van Gogh's paintings. This was because, without knowing it, the artist himself had made things simple for the forger! Van Gogh painted over 2,000 works and left most of them unsigned. Since he did not sell many paintings while he was alive, there were few official records, or provenances, of them.

Van Gogh's sister-in-law inherited all of his paintings after his death. She sold them mainly to Paul Cassirer, a famous art dealer. When Cassirer was fooled by Wacker's fake van Goghs, Wacker thought he had succeeded. It wasn't long, however, before his "van Goghs" were identified as fakes, and he landed in jail.

THE TRIAL OF OTTO WACKER–AKG-IMAGES/ULLSTEIN BILD

BUT WHY?

The timing was perfect. Wacker planned his scam right at the start of the van Gogh craze in 1928. No one wanted van Gogh's work while he was alive, but almost 40 years after his death, people were willing to pay a lot of money for one of his paintings.

> **?** Which other artists or musicians became more famous after they died? Why is this?

AND HOW?

Wacker got his brother Leonhard, an art restorer and painter, to create all the forged pieces. Art dealers were so eager to make money that they weren't as careful as they should have been when examining the fakes. In one provenance, Wacker claimed that the paintings had belonged to a mysterious Russian aristocrat. The experts were so excited that they never asked for more proof.

> **?** What steps could today's artists take as they paint to ensure that the provenances of their work can be trusted?

aristocrat: *member of the upper class*

EXPOSED!

Some of Wacker's fakes were first discovered during a 1928 van Gogh exhibition. They looked pretty bad when they were hanging next to the real van Goghs. Experts soon realized that there were 33 fakes on the official list of van Gogh's work. When all the fakes led to Wacker, he was charged with fraud.

AS A RESULT ...

Otto Wacker fooled some pretty important people. It was very embarrassing for the experts involved. Experts around the world are still fighting about the real and fake van Goghs. More and more fakes are being exposed.

Quick Fact

Vincent van Gogh only sold one painting during his lifetime! He gave most of his work to friends and family. Because there are no records of these gifts, it is quite easy for forgers to make up stories about where their "van Goghs" came from.

Many of Vincent van Gogh's paintings have sold for record-breaking prices. In 1990, his Portrait of Dr. Gachet *sold for $82.5 million!*

10

GET REAL!

Read this comparison chart and become a van Gogh fraud-buster!

Take a closer look at:	Signs of a REAL van Gogh:	Signs of a FAKE:
Imprints on the paint	Imprints of canvases can be seen across the entire painting surface. This is because of van Gogh's unusual habit of placing wet paintings on top of one another.	Most forgeries have only small canvas imprints. These are meant to give the impression that newly painted pictures have been placed on top of one another.
Color and brushstrokes	The colors of his genuine later works are always fresh and clear. They gleam and shine because he always applied paint to his canvases quickly in a single, uninterrupted flow. His strokes are sure and confident.	All the forgeries feature muddied colors. They do not give the impression of spontaneous, energetic marks of color. The strokes seem hesitant, labored, and indecisive.
Cracking	Van Gogh never worked with layers of color. Because of his one-shot method, his art was never affected by craquelure. *craquelure: small cracks that form on an old painting*	The paint on all the forged canvases shows craquelure. Layers of paint drying at different times create these cracks and so are never found in genuine works by van Gogh.

The Expert Says...

No catalog of [van Gogh's] work, no publication of his letters, no record prices, and no major exhibitions netted him so much publicity as the Wacker scandal.

— Walter Feilchenfeldt, leading van Gogh expert

Take Note

Otto Wacker makes our list even though he never forged a painting in his life! He commissioned fakes, and he was successful in damaging the confidence of buyers and exposing the "experts" as a club of arrogant people.

• Do you think Wacker's brother, Leonhard, who is thought to have painted the fakes, should be on this list? Why or why not?

5   4   3   2   1

9 TOM KEATING

Keating's interest in art developed at a young age. Because his family was poor, he made his own paintbrushes out of feathers he found on dead birds.

TOM KEATING—GETTY IMAGES

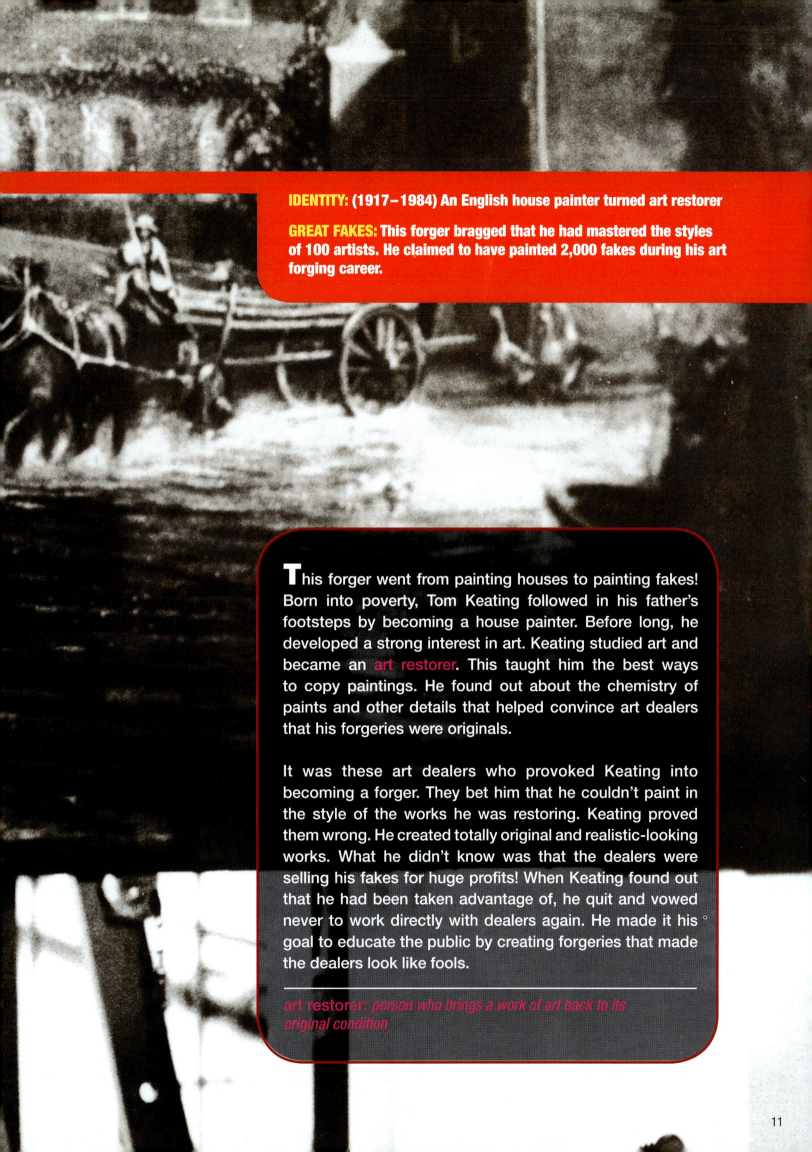

IDENTITY: (1917–1984) An English house painter turned art restorer

GREAT FAKES: This forger bragged that he had mastered the styles of 100 artists. He claimed to have painted 2,000 fakes during his art forging career.

This forger went from painting houses to painting fakes! Born into poverty, Tom Keating followed in his father's footsteps by becoming a house painter. Before long, he developed a strong interest in art. Keating studied art and became an art restorer. This taught him the best ways to copy paintings. He found out about the chemistry of paints and other details that helped convince art dealers that his forgeries were originals.

It was these art dealers who provoked Keating into becoming a forger. They bet him that he couldn't paint in the style of the works he was restoring. Keating proved them wrong. He created totally original and realistic-looking works. What he didn't know was that the dealers were selling his fakes for huge profits! When Keating found out that he had been taken advantage of, he quit and vowed never to work directly with dealers again. He made it his goal to educate the public by creating forgeries that made the dealers look like fools.

art restorer: *person who brings a work of art back to its original condition*

11

TOM KEATING

BUT WHY?

Keating felt art dealers were cheats and wanted to make fools of them with his fakes. He also made forgeries because of his love for art. He loved the paintings of old masters and even said that he sometimes felt himself being taken over by the spirits of those great artists.

Quick Fact

Tom Keating created his own sepia (brown-colored) ink by simmering walnuts in water for 10 hours. Keating used this walnut ink to make "Rembrandt" drawings, knowing that it would fade with time and reveal the drawings as fakes.

AND HOW?

Keating knew that the backs of old frames from auction houses had numbers on them. He bought these frames secondhand. Then, he found out which artist a certain number represented and painted a picture to go in the frame in the style of that artist. Keating also processed his own special paints. With the help of his girlfriend, Jane Kelly, he displayed his works to dealers and at auctions.

Quick Fact

Keating painted swear words or "this is a fake" in lead white under his paintings so that any X-ray would reveal they were forgeries. He wanted the art experts to be ashamed at how easily they had been fooled.

EXPOSED!

Geraldine Norman, a journalist for *The Times* of London, wrote a story about 13 fake Samuel Palmer watercolor paintings. After the article was published, people said that Tom Keating was the forger. Norman named Keating as the forger in her second article. He phoned and told her she had been right all along!

AS A RESULT ...

Art dealers and auction houses were horrified when Keating revealed just how many paintings he had forged during his 20-year career. Those directly involved were angry and lashed out at the media and Keating.

? Why do you think that dealers would be unwilling to reveal they had unknowingly purchased forgeries?

Tom Keating with one of his fakes

10   9   8

UNDER THE HAMMER

Find out what happened to this expert faker in this British <mark>newspaper article</mark>.

From "The Faker's Moll," by Matthew Sweet, *The Independent*, January 13, 1999

... The artist under the hammer is Tom Keating, the flamboyant faker who, in the sixties and seventies, used his talent for *mimicry* to make fools of the saleroom [showroom] establishment and a very comfortable living for himself.

Since Keating's death in 1984, his fakes have acquired a market value of their own. In 1989, his version of Turner's *Fighting Temeraire* sold for £27,500 [around $55,000] ... . Among the 85 lots [on auction] are pictures imitating Degas, Matisse, Modigliani, and the English visionary painter Samuel Palmer, as well as original works that reveal Keating's own style. They are being sold by Brad Maurice, widower of Jane Kelly, Keating's former girlfriend ... She was also his business manager, lover, housekeeper, and partner in crime.

In 1979, they were both arrested after their sale of a series of fake Samuel Palmer landscapes was exposed by the journalist Geraldine Norman, then saleroom correspondent of *The Times*. The trial was the object of intense interest: Jane turned *Queen's Evidence* and was given an 18-month suspended sentence. Keating pleaded not guilty, and when the case was dropped because of his poor health, he emerged from the courtroom a celebrity. His autobiography, *The Fake's Progress* (co-written with Norman and her husband, Frank), was widely read. In the eighties, he completed two series for Channel 4 and made a fortune from a high-profile auction of his phoney old masters, although a fatal heart attack in 1984 ensured that he didn't live to spend the cash.

mimicry: *art of imitating others*
Queen's Evidence: *in England, evidence against the person on trial*

> What Keating did was illegal, but instead of paying a price for his crime, he got a TV show and a book deal. What makes fakes and the way they are made so interesting?

The Expert Says...

" To paint a picture in the manner of Rembrandt, to sign it, to distress it so that it appears old ... none of this is a crime. ... The problem with the law comes when you sell it. "

— Geraldine Norman, co-author of *The Fake's Progress*, and the reporter who identified Tom Keating as the Samuel Palmer forger

Take Note

Tom Keating stands at #9 on our list. Although he probably earned the least amount of money of any of the forgers on our list, he forged a lot of paintings.

- Who should be held accountable when art buyers are fooled? The "artist"? The dealers? The auctioneers? Why?

KARL SIM

Karl Sim uses this prop as a joke during his speeches about life as a forger.

KARL SIM–COURTESY KARL SIM

IDENTITY: Born in 1923, this New Zealander began forging fairly late in life, at the age of 43.

GREAT FAKES: Though he specialized in forging the works of Charles Frederick Goldie, a famous painter from New Zealand, Sim has also admitted to forging works in the styles of 78 other artists.

This forger says he's had "more lives than a cat" and we believe it! He's been a real estate agent, a salesman, an auctioneer, and a wine maker. Of course, it is Sim's fake paintings that finally got him noticed in New Zealand and around the world.

These fakes also got Sim in trouble with the law. But he didn't mind. Sim has been known to call the police "the demons." We know he's wrong, but he has also said that he didn't think tricking rich people was a crime! This guy got a thrill out of having the upper hand. His fakes let him outsmart the police — but only for a little while …

Eventually, Sim was caught and convicted of 20 counts of forgery and 18 counts of uttering. Amazingly, he never served a day in jail. He was given 200 hours of community work and a $1,000 fine. He now says his forging days are over. These days, he takes great delight in appearing on TV, speaking at art openings, and giving talks to any interested audience.

uttering: *crime of selling something that you know is fake*

KARL SIM

BUT WHY?

From a young age, Sim scraped out a living any way he could. He found forgery easy and every good sale motivated him to keep on copying.

AND HOW?

Sim had a little help starting out. As a student, one of his friends helped him forge the signatures of famous artists. The friend gave these paintings to an auction house where they all sold. It was the start of Sim's newest career.

Quick Fact

After Karl Sim was charged, he had his name officially changed to Carl Feodor Goldie. This way he could legally sign his works "C.F. Goldie" — the same signature as that of the artist he copied the most.

In this self-portrait, Sim shows himself surrounded by the signatures of many of the artists whose work he forged.

EXPOSED!

He may have been a great artist, but Sim's spelling wasn't very good. He made mistakes on several of the signatures on his forgeries — not surprisingly, people started to get suspicious. Dealers also caught on when they noticed that a huge number of forgeries were coming out of the tiny village of Foxton where Sim had his auction house.

AS A RESULT ...

New Zealand's artistic history is so young that it is considered a patriotic act to own original Kiwi, or New Zealand, art. Sim copied the work of famous artists from New Zealand. Art experts claim that Sim has sabotaged the artistic heritage of his own country by forging the work of its great artists.

? What paintings are part of your country's artistic heritage? How would you feel if you found out someone had secretly added phony works to your national gallery?

The Expert Says ...

"While we ... do not endorse forgery in any way, there is no doubt that Sim/Goldie's notoriety has made the average person in New Zealand more aware of our unique cultural heritage.

— Rebecca Sharpe, art dealer, owner of Artworks Gallery and proud promoter of original New Zealand art

Quick Fact

Karl Sim was drafted into the army at 18. While he was there, his artistic talents earned him the job of creating camouflage patterns for jungle warfare.

PURE GOLDIE

Learn about the real Charles Frederick Goldie in this <mark>profile</mark>.

One of Sim's earliest forgeries was of Charles Frederick Goldie's painting *Ina Te Papatahi from 1910.*

Charles Frederick Goldie, the real artist (the one Sim loved to forge), was born in Auckland, New Zealand, in 1870. He showed promise as an artist at an early age and was sent to Paris to study at the Académie Julian and at the École des Beaux-Arts. There, Goldie developed into a realist, drawing the things he saw as realistically as possible.

Goldie dedicated himself to drawing and painting detailed portraits of Pakeha (Pa-kee-haw), or white people, and Maori (Mah-aw-ree). The Maori were people who traveled to New Zealand more than a thousand years ago. He especially liked to paint Maori with moko (elaborate facial tattoos), dressed in costumes, and posed with sorrowful expressions. It was a common, but incorrect, belief at this time that the Maori were a dying race.

Many people loved the portraits. However, some critics said they were like colored photographs — too realistic. They said that Goldie was creating a false picture of the Maori by dressing them up instead of showing what they actually wore. The sad expressions and slumped poses of his models made them look defeated and depressed.

Some people see exhibitions of Goldie's works as shrines to Maori ancestors. Others still believe that Charles Frederick Goldie used his brush to put down the Maori and to express his own prejudice toward the Maori people.

---

prejudice: *unreasonable opinions or attitudes of a hostile nature*

Take Note

Karl Sim stands at #8 on our list because his crimes mostly affected only New Zealand. If they had had more global impact, he might have ranked higher.
- Why might it have been easier for Sim to get away with forgery than someone who lived in Europe or North America?

5   4   3   2   1

7 JOHN MYATT

After he got out of jail, Myatt started a successful business called Genuine Fakes. He paints forgeries of famous works for his clients. Since Myatt signs his own name to the copies (and not the original artist's name), what he does is perfectly legal.

IDENTITY: Born in 1945, this Englishman was a mild-mannered high-school teacher and local church choir director!

GREAT FAKES: He forged 200 works in the styles of nine modern masters. He now runs a successful (and legal!) forgery business.

Go to his Web site, fill out an order form, and John Myatt will paint you the masterpiece of your dreams! He did hard time for his crime of forgery, and now Myatt uses his talents to live on the right side of the law.

Myatt didn't start out as a success story, though. He was a frustrated artist who was never able to sell any of his own work. He worked as an art teacher to pay the bills. When he met John Drewe in 1986, Myatt finally found the recognition and money he always wanted — too bad it was as a forger. Read on to find out how this duo pulled off a scam that lasted nine years …

JOHN MYATT

BUT WHY?

Myatt might say his troubles made him do it. His wife left him with two small children and the money he made as a teacher was stretched very thin. Myatt placed an ad in the paper advertising his skills at imitating the masters of modern art. He never intended to fool anyone into thinking they were real, but John Drewe had other plans!

AND HOW?

John Drewe was a fast-talking con artist. He told Myatt he wanted the fake paintings to decorate his home. Once he saw the quality of Myatt's work, Drewe knew he could sell them to museums. Myatt knew it was wrong, but decided to cooperate because of the money.

? How do Myatt's reasons for forging compare to Drewe's? As you read, notice what makes these forgers choose a life of crime.

EXPOSED!

When John Drewe's wife gave police *incriminating* documents about the forgeries, Myatt didn't have much of a choice but to confess. Just before he was arrested, Myatt had actually written a letter to Drewe saying that he wanted out of the scam. The police found the letter and as Myatt said, it "more or less amounted to a signed confession."

AS A RESULT ...

Experts were sloppy and put all their trust in the provenances that Drewe gave them. They were also greedy and jumped at the chance to own rare paintings. Yet again, people lost confidence in the world of art experts, auction houses, and museums.

incriminating: *showing proof of a crime*

> During his four months in prison, Myatt earned the nickname "Picasso" because he painted portraits of his fellow inmates.

Quick Fact

Each of Myatt's new "Genuine Fake" forgeries has a microchip implanted within it so that owners cannot later claim they are real.

The Expert Says...

"[Many collectors' interests in art] are reflections of social climbing and romanticism about names, a thousand things that have nothing to do with the surface of the work of art."

— Geraldine Norman, British art journalist, credited with exposing forgers Tom Keating and Eric Hebborn

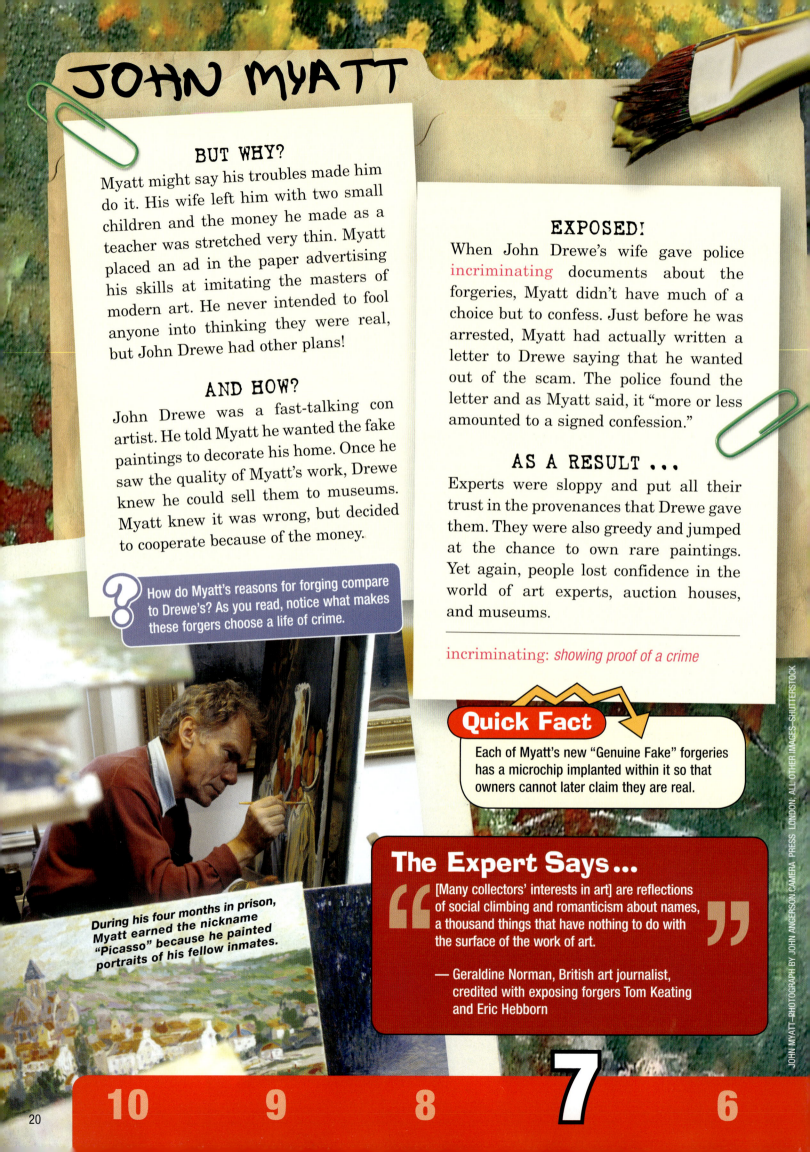

ARTIST FOR HIRE!

Get the whole story in this ==descriptive account== of John Myatt's career as a forger.

It was John Myatt's ad in a London newspaper that first attracted the attention of "Professor" John Drewe. Over two years, Drewe bought 14 paintings from Myatt. Then, in 1986, he told Myatt that a huge auction house in London had offered $38,000 for one of Myatt's small paintings. "That was the moment that the legitimate business stopped and the crime began," Myatt later admitted.

Over the next seven years, as the scam continued, Myatt earned just a little less than he would have as a teacher, but he got to stay home with his children. Drewe, on the other hand, made about $4 million.

Myatt himself says his fakes were not very good. He used ordinary house paint instead of oils, and his technique wasn't always perfect. The simplest of scientific tests would have immediately shown his works to be fakes. Myatt relied on the fact that authorities could never scientifically analyze every single one of his paintings because of the huge costs and amount of time these tests take.

A year before his arrest, after forging 200 paintings, Myatt became depressed and stopped the forgeries. He felt he was in too deep and was worried about what the future might hold. "It was shocking; it quite terrified me," Myatt once said in an interview. "The moment they started to restore them they would know what they were faced with."

After serving only four months for conspiracy to defraud, Myatt was released and he started his "legal forgery" business. Now, two movies are being made about his criminal past. Myatt has been hired to create all the paintings for the movies.

Quick Fact

Aside from being an art teacher, John Myatt wrote a hit song called "Silly Games." In 1979, the song made the British top 40.

Take Note

We've placed John Myatt higher on this list than Karl Sim because he was half of the team that pulled off the greatest art scam in history. Myatt and his partner, John Drewe, #3, fooled the world's top art dealers and sold paintings to the world's most respected auction houses. The team scammed people out of millions of dollars.

- Why do you think some people buy "genuine fakes"? Would you? Why or why not?

5 4 3 2 1

6 GUY HAIN

A copy of Auguste Rodin's famous bronze sculpture The Thinker, seen here in St. Paul, France

IMAGE–SHUTTERSTOCK

IDENTITY: This French art dealer went from being an honest salesperson to selling fake sculptures.

GREAT FAKES: He forged more than 6,000 bronze sculptures worth close to $38 million.

An interest in bronze sculptures turned into a criminal career when Guy Hain (Gey Hen) started making and selling copies of history's most famous bronzes. No one would have imagined that a man who sold veterinary products would end up as the mastermind behind one of the biggest forgery rings in the history of French art.

When Hain was fired from his job as a salesman, he decided to try his hand at a new sales career dealing in art. In 1962, after buying a small bronze sculpture by Auguste Rodin (O-goost Roh-dahn), Hain got an idea for a new venture. He opened a successful art gallery in a posh area of Paris. There, he learned more about sculpture. He learned even more about how much people were willing to pay for bronzes. This gave Hain an idea.

After eight years, Hain closed the gallery and learned everything he needed to know about metal casting and making bronze sculptures. With this new knowledge, his experience in sales, and his contacts in the art world, he was ready to make his ill-gotten fortune.

---

ill-gotten: *gained in an illegal or dishonest way*

GUY HAIN

BUT WHY?

It's not a good reason but it's a popular one: money. The market for bronzes was so good when Hain was in business that he easily became a very rich man.

AND HOW?

Fake sculptures are far harder to detect than forgeries of paintings, so Hain was able to fool the experts for a very long time. French law allows artists to make 12 copies of a sculpture, number each one, and legally call all 12 pieces originals. Any more copies have to be marked "reproduction." Hain made extra bronzes using the original molds, gave them the right signatures, but didn't mark them as reproductions. Nobody knew which 12 were the real originals. Hain made a fortune selling a ton of fakes!

Quick Fact
The number 12 was chosen because the molds start to wear down after that and the quality of the sculptures gets worse.

The Expert Says...

" They act as if the living presence of the artist is not necessary to create art … . When he died, the right to sign his name died with him. "

— Gary Arseneau, artist and art dealer, sharing his opinion on people's right to make original sculptures after an artist has died

EXPOSED!

In 1992, Guy Hain's time was up! Inspector Vincenot of the Dijon investigative police had just solved a case involving fake Alberto Giacometti sculptures. Hain was next on his list! He was arrested and approximately 2,500 molds and bronzes were confiscated, or removed, from his studio. That's a lot of evidence!

Quick Fact
Authorities believe that Guy Hain copied the works of over 98 different artists.

AS A RESULT ...

Police have identified over 1,000 of Hain's fakes but fear that there are still about 6,000 sculptures by Hain circulating as originals. Sadly, all French bronzes from the late 19th and early 20th centuries are now under suspicion of being forgeries.

8

6

THE ART OF THE SCAM

This step-by-step guide shows how a sculpture is made and how Hain took advantage of the complex world of sculpting.

SCULPTING 101

- First, the sculptor creates a small clay model, called a maquette (mah-ket).

- Plaster casts, or molds, of the sculpture are then made (sometimes this is done by an assistant).

- Then the castings are made at a foundry. This is where bronze will be poured into the casts to get the final product. Remember, this can be done up to 12 different times for one sculpture.

- Next comes chasing (polishing the surface to remove imperfections) and applying the patina (a gold coating often found on old bronze). This may be done at different foundries.

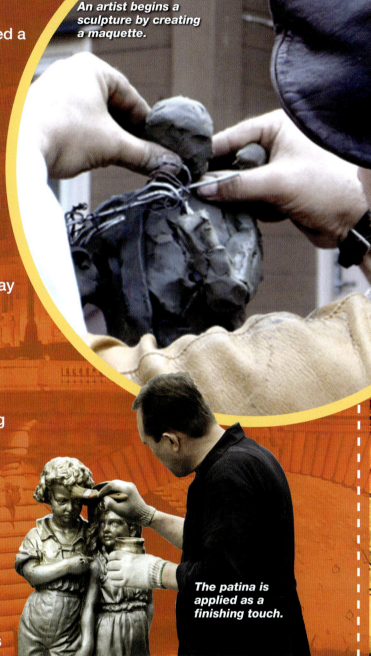

An artist begins a sculpture by creating a maquette.

The patina is applied as a finishing touch.

HAIN'S PERFECT SCAM

- Hain taught himself everything about metal casting and foundries.

- He made friends with George Rudier, the son of the man who cast sculptures for Rodin.

- Hain bought his own chasing shop and foundry.

- Hain used George Rudier's mark so that people would think they were getting one of Rodin's 12 originals.

- He made casts from the artist's original maquettes (you can buy these at foundries).

- Hain marked the sculptures with the dead artist's signature and founder's marks even though he didn't own them.

- Hain didn't let 18 months in jail stop him. After he got out of prison, he went right back to forging.

Take Note

Police estimate that 6,000 of his forgeries are still out there in the hands of unsuspecting buyers. Guy Hain stands at #6 on our list for the sheer number of forgeries he made.
- Compare Guy Hain's methods of deception to those of John Myatt, #7 on our list. Who do you think was more devious or deceitful? Explain your answer.

? Which do you think would be easier to copy, a painting or a sculpture? Why?

5   4   3   2   1

Elmyr de Hory's talent for imitating Picasso became his ticket to a life of crime.

IDENTITY: (1906–1976) Elmyr de Hory's (El-meer duh Hoar-ey) career as a forger spanned 30 years.

GREAT FAKES: De Hory's imitations of modern masters made him famous. Some of his best forgeries were of works by Edgar Degas, Pablo Picasso, and Henri Matisse.

Born into a wealthy Hungarian family, Elmyr de Hory went from living a life of privilege to being a penniless prisoner. As a young man during World War II, de Hory was thrown into a Nazi concentration camp. He daringly escaped. But once de Hory was free, he learned that his parents had been killed and his family's fortune was completely gone.

The war gave de Hory the perfect backdrop for his crime. He pretended to be a Hungarian aristocrat who had lost all of his money during the war and needed to sell his pricey art collection. In 1946, he started copying and selling fake Picassos. De Hory was brilliant at painting, but when it came to choosing business partners, he wasn't quite as good. His partners made a fortune selling his works and deliberately kept de Hory poor to make sure that he would keep painting fakes.

As his career turned sour, his paintings became less perfect and the police started to become more and more suspicious of Elmyr de Hory …

 De Hory began his forging career shortly after the war. How much do you think the war contributed to his success as a forger?

ELMYR DE HORY–TIME LIFE PICTURES/GETTY IMAGES

ELMYR DE HORY

BUT WHY?

After losing his parents and all his money, de Hory had to find a way to support himself. At first, he tried to make an honest living by trying to sell the original works of art that he painted. He soon found, though, that his work didn't sell. His fake "Picassos" and "Chagalls," on the other hand, sold for plenty!

AND HOW?

The war gave de Hory the perfect opportunity to sell fakes to dealers eager to restock their collections. Dishonest art dealers who knew his secret also helped sell his fakes to important collectors and museums. De Hory avoided arousing suspicion by using pseudonyms, or fake names, and by never living in one place for too long.

Noah and the Rainbow, by Marc Chagall — is it real? Who knows!

EXPOSED!

Remember those business partners who helped de Hory when he was starting out? Well, they became increasingly greedy and tried to make as much money as they could by flooding the market with his fakes. Bad idea! The FBI started to connect the dots and closed in on de Hory.

AS A RESULT ...

The scandal around de Hory's fakes involved many people who made their reputations as art experts. After the fakes were discovered, questions were raised about what actually gives someone true expertise. Once again, a scandal in the art world forced experts to use more scientific methods to test paintings. Today, experts use X-rays, ultraviolet light, and microscopes to test the age of paintings.

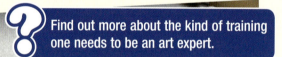

? Find out more about the kind of training one needs to be an art expert.

Elmyr de Hory standing next to one of his forged Matisse drawings

Quick Fact

Ironically, de Hory's fake "masterpieces" are now considered valuable collector's items. De Hory fakes now sell for tens of thousands of dollars!

DE HORY'S DEALS

De Hory's toxic business connections helped to spread his fakes around the globe. But he was overworked and underpaid! Read all about it in this flow chart.

Elmyr de Hory

De Hory had some toxic business relationships ...

Jacques Chamberlin

De Hory's first dealer for almost a year in 1946. De Hory ended the relationship when he learned Chamberlin was cheating him.

Fernand Legros

By the 1950s, de Hory realized he hated selling his own work. He happily hired Legros, who thought he deserved half of the profits.

Réal Lessard

This young French-Canadian helped Legros rip off de Hory. The dangerous duo kept de Hory working nonstop on the island of Ibiza, Spain. They gave him a small allowance and took the rest of his money.

Algur H. Meadows

This wealthy Texas oilman bought 56 of de Hory's forgeries from Legros. When he found out they were fakes, he was enraged and demanded that Legros be prosecuted.

Orson Welles

With Clifford Irving, Orson Welles (one of the most famous filmmakers of the 20th century) produced a documentary about de Hory called *F for Fake* (1974). Earlier in his career, Welles terrorized thousands of radio listeners with a broadcast that faked an alien invasion.

Clifford Irving

In 1969, Irving wrote a book about de Hory called *Fake!* A year later, Irving created a "forgery" of his own — a fake autobiography of Howard Hughes. He thought he could get away with it because Hughes had become a recluse, but Hughes spoke up and created a huge scandal.

recluse: *someone who lives in isolation, away from others*

The Expert Says ...

"His range was so big. He could paint so many different artists. ... Some people who bought [de Hory paintings] know they are fakes, but don't want to look foolish."

— Peter Wright, owner, San Francisco's Terrain Gallery

Take Note

Elmyr de Hory sits at #5 on our list. His talent puts him higher than Hain. He also became famous enough as a forger to be the subject of a best-selling book and a 1974 Orson Welles documentary.

• Compare de Hory's story with that of Tom Keating. Both of these forgers became famous because of their illegal scams. Explain why this does or doesn't surprise you.

5   4   3   2   1

4 ERIC HEBBORN

He could draw, paint, and even sculpt like the experts!

IDENTITY: (1934–1996) Born in England, Eric Hebborn was a troublemaker right from the beginning.

GREAT FAKES: He bragged that his forgeries had been bought by some of the most famous museums in the world.

There seemed little doubt that it was murder. On January 11, 1996, Eric Hebborn was found dead on a street in Rome, Italy. Was it an angry lover or a mugging gone wrong — or was it because he was about to reveal how many of his forgeries hung in the world's most famous museums?

It is thought that many museum curators and art dealers breathed a sigh of relief that morning. In the world of art experts, reputation is everything. But now that Hebborn was dead, he would never be able to say who had bought his fakes or whom he had fooled.

Before he died, Hebborn had an appointment to meet two art experts in Rome. They were going to watch him recreate a drawing by the artist Piranesi (Pee-rah-nay-see). This way, the experts would learn once and for all if the art their museum had bought for $28,500 was a forgery. Hebborn's art dealer canceled the meeting and told the artist not to do the drawing. The next morning, Hebborn's body was discovered. Suspicious?

? This mystery was never solved. If you were investigating, whom would you question?

31

ERIC HEBBORN

BUT WHY?

Hebborn loved art and was a gifted artist. However, he was not a big fan of art experts. He called them greedy creatures "for whom a work of art is as good or bad as the amount it fetches." These feelings inspired him to create forgeries that would make the experts look bad.

AND HOW?

Instead of copying a famous drawing or painting, Hebborn created a "new" one in the same style as the artist. He then said that it had just been discovered. Eric used household items like olive oil, coffee, and smoke to make his fakes look old.

Quick Fact

Hebborn sold finished paintings as well as unfinished sketches. Now that Hebborn is dead, experts have no one who can say for sure whether or not they've identified the fakes.

EXPOSED!

Hebborn was found out when a curator noticed strange similarities between two works of art. Both had been bought from the same art dealer. They were supposed to be by different artists, but the curator noticed that they were painted on the same type of canvas and in the same style. Both works were traced back to Hebborn. Although he admitted to his crime in his autobiography, *Drawn to Trouble: Confessions of a Master Forger*, Hebborn wasn't brought to trial before his death in 1996.

? Why would someone confess to a crime in a book? Give some reasons.

AS A RESULT ...

Eric Hebborn made so many convincing fakes that his full impact on the art world may never be known. Because he died before naming names, art dealers were able to protect their reputations. Unfortunately, this meant that many of Hebborn's fakes were never discovered or exposed.

? Why is it so hard for some art experts to admit they've made a mistake?

MASTER FAKER

Here's some advice straight from *The Art Forger's Handbook,* Hebborn's how-to book on making forgeries. Check out his account in this excerpt …

When we offer our wares [forgeries] to a dealer who specializes in drawings and paintings, we are often challenging a very knowledgeable person who may be considered an expert as well as a merchant, especially by themselves … Certainly, trying to do business with a rapacious dealer is a much more harrowing experience than dealing with the gentle, disinterested scholar!

The best possible way of introducing yourself to a dealer is as a customer. Dealers adore customers, and once you have achieved this status you will always be given a warm welcome. Buying from them also ensures that you will get to know their stock, what kind of pictures they like and what prices they will ask for them. This last point is very important because it will help you to establish their mark-up. Dealers generally get a good proportion of their stock from auction rooms and if you have been following the saleroom's activities you are quite likely to see something on their walls that sold recently at auction. Consequently, you know what they paid for it.

Another way of getting to know a dealer (and in any case better than just walking in off the street) is to pretend they have been recommended to you by some important person in the trade or in the museum world. … A little flattery goes a long way with dealers. By the same token they are very touchy about criticism. … Keep quiet, and let them decide what it is you have for sale.

rapacious: *greedy*
harrowing: *stressful*

The Expert Says…

"He was seen by some as a hero, but he wasn't a hero … Hebborn was a killer of art."

— Eduardo Testori, Italian art dealer

Take Note

Eric Hebborn ranks #4. He created over 1,000 fakes and was a master of many art styles. Hebborn's fakes fooled the world's top experts. The fact that he was murdered hours before he could reveal who had purchased his fake paintings adds an extra element of drama to his story.

- Do you think it's possible to ever know what's real and what's fake in the museums Hebborn was about to expose? Why or why not?

4   3   2   1

Experts say that Drewe faked the provenances of many modern works of art. No one can be 100 percent sure about which ones are forged and which ones are real.

IDENTITY: Born in 1948, this British man is known as the mastermind behind the biggest modern art fraud of the 20th century.

GREAT FAKES: This great faker has never even picked up a paintbrush! Instead he forged hundreds of provenances, stating that fake paintings were actually real.

John Drewe is a wacky guy who has lied for much of his life. He once claimed he was a descendant of the Earl of York! He also got a high-ranking job by pretending to be a physics expert. In 1986, he found John Myatt (#7 on our list), the high-school art teacher who advertised that he could create fakes of modern art. While Myatt did not intend to deceive anyone, Drewe had other plans …

Over the next 10 years, John Drewe created hundreds of lies, false identities, and forged documents. All of these were used to convince buyers that Myatt's paintings were actually works by some of the greatest modern-day artists. The sales of Myatt's fakes eventually totaled more than $4 million and threw the art world into chaos.

JOHN DREWE

BUT WHY?

Greed! Drewe knew art dealers would pay big money for works by famous artists and he wanted to cash in. The provenances that he made up were very elaborate. He felt like a genius when he successfully tricked so-called art experts!

AND HOW?

Drewe had the brains and John Myatt had the artistic talent — together they made a very successful team. Myatt painted over 200 fakes for this scam. Drewe created fake documents for each fake painting. These papers, including fake sales receipts, fake letters from art experts, and fake letters from previous owners persuaded dealers that the paintings were real. By making large donations to various museums, Drewe gained access to official libraries and files. Drewe stole, forged, and copied whatever he could.

EXPOSED!

It was Drewe's ex-girlfriend who eventually told the police about his crimes. The police found all the tools Drewe had used to make fake documents at his house. They found two stolen gallery catalogs on his kitchen table, rubber "authentication seal" stamps, and hundreds of documents from the Victoria and Albert Museum and the Tate Gallery (now Tate Britain). On February 15, 1999, Drewe was sentenced to six years in jail.

> **?** If you had been the judge, what sentence would you have given Drewe?

AS A RESULT ...

To prevent forgeries like John Drewe's from happening again, many museums and libraries have tightened their security and access policies. Drewe's fakes also exposed problems at large auction houses — they should have checked their art more thoroughly. Police have recovered 73 of the forged paintings, but more than 125 buyers still don't know that their treasures are fakes.

The Expert Says...

" Corrupting such material damages not only the individual item, but inevitably undermines and taints the whole system. "

— John Bevan, the lawyer who successfully prosecuted John Drewe in 1999

taints: *spoils; ruins*

ALL IMAGES—SHUTTERSTOCK

10   9   8   7   6

THE PERFECT CON

1. As you know, Drewe got Myatt to paint the fakes. The next step for Drewe was to get into the National Art Library at the Victoria and Albert Museum in London. Once inside, he took apart the Ohana Gallery catalog. Then he added new pages that were printed on identical paper. These pages had photos of the forgeries and fake provenances that Drewe had created. He then re-stitched the catalog and put it back on the shelf. When experts found the information on the painting in the catalog, they were convinced they were real.

2. Drewe also created a fake company called Art Research Associates. He hired some salespeople to help sell his fake paintings to dealers. He then hired himself out as an art expert, Professor Drewe. His job was to investigate provenances and reassure clients that the works they wanted to buy were real. He even took them to the National Art Library and showed them the catalog he had forged. If the buyers needed more proof, he had that covered — see step #3!

3. Drewe forged official-looking letters by reworking an existing signature and putting it on a lawyer's letterhead, or official letter paper. One fake letter read:

To Whom It May Concern,
This letter confirms the painting by Giacometti is being sold with the full authority of the owner.

The supposed owner was Len Martin, a man who did not exist!

Quick Fact

Alberto Giacometti (Gee-ah-coh-meh-ti) was a Swiss surrealist painter and sculptor. His work was very imaginative and original and aimed at expressing the subconscious.

Take Note

Even though he never painted, John Drewe is #3 because of his ability to deceive dealers with fake histories. Many dealers have admitted that even when they had doubts about a painting being real, Drewe's fake documents and provenances were so convincing that they believed him.

- The reputations of the art experts who were conned by John Drewe were ruined. Because they were careless, they made it possible for tons of fakes to be hung in museums. What do you think they had to do to reassure the public and regain their reputation? Would you believe them?

5   **3**   2   1

Han van Meegeren painting a replica of a Vermeer in court to prove that he could actually do it

IMAGE–AKG-IMAGES/ULLSTEIN BILD

GEREN

Han van Meegeren (Hahn vahn Me-grr-n) thought of himself as an artist. However, art critics did not think much of his work. Van Meegeren felt insulted and started to fake paintings as a way to get back at the art critics. He experimented with ways to fake the age of paint. He searched for old canvases and frames.

In 1937, van Meegeren forged a painting by Johannes Vermeer. It was so good that Abraham Bredius, the world expert on the works of Vermeer, said it was "every inch a Vermeer" when he saw it. When this happened, van Meegeren knew he could fool anyone! Soon his fake painting was hanging in Rotterdam's famous Boijmans Museum. Now that he was able to fool the experts, van Meegeren was well on his way to becoming a successful forger. Van Meegeren made the equivalent of millions of dollars in fewer than 10 years working as a forger.

BUT WHY?

Van Meegeren's original paintings did not sell because his style of painting was not popular. By forging Vermeer's work, he made lots of money and got revenge against the art experts who criticized his original works.

AND HOW?

Van Meegeren bought genuinely old, but unimportant, paintings and scraped off the pictures so he could use the real 17th century canvases as backdrops. He mixed his own paints and made his own brushes. To give his works the old, crackled look they needed to appear real, he baked them in a special oven.

? Van Meegeren spent four years perfecting this process. Do you think it is easier to forge a new work of art or an old work of art? What details would the artist have to worry about?

EXPOSED!

In 1945, van Meegeren's story took an amazing turn. He was accused of selling a genuine Vermeer painting to a Nazi, Hermann Goering. The Dutch police arrested van Meegeren for selling a national treasure to the enemy. Faced with the death penalty if found guilty, van Meegeren had to confess that he had actually sold a fake. To prove it, he painted another fake right in the courtroom!

AS A RESULT ...

The art world started relying on science, instead of just opinion, to discover a painting's origin. Today, paintings are X-rayed to see what lies beneath their top layer. Scientists test the paint and canvas of a painting before deciding whether or not it is real. Even with all these tests, some fakes still manage to fool the experts!

Van Meegeren at his trial

Quick Fact
Because van Meegeren traded his fake Vermeer to the Nazi Hermann Goering for 200 real Dutch paintings, he felt he should have been called Holland's hero, not the country's traitor.

? The Nazis are known to have stolen lots of important and expensive original works of art during World War II. What do you think happened to these real paintings?

10   9   8   7   6

Faking It

A step-by-step guide to the PERFECT van Meegeren forgery

1. Find a cheap painting from the 17th century.

2. Use a pumice stone to remove the paint from the canvas (now you have a canvas from the right time period).

3. Apply a primer coat to prepare the surface for painting.

4. Use only pigments that were available during the time of the original artist.

5. Grind the pigments by hand and mix them with ambertol, turpentine, and oil of lilac. This gives the painting an old-looking finish.

6. Construct badger hair brushes, just as Vermeer used to use. Modern bristles left in the painting would be a dead giveaway of a fake.

7. Start painting!

pumice stone: *porous form of volcanic glass used for smoothing or polishing*
pigments: *ingredients used to give color*
ambertol: *synthetic resin used to make varnishes, inks, etc.*

8. Bake the finished painting for one hour at 140°F in a special oven. This will give it the old-fashioned crackled look.

9. Varnish the painting and let it dry.

10. Time to add some more cracks. Gently poke the back of the painting with a broom handle.

11. Fake the look of years of dust filling in the cracks by rubbing ink across the painting. Rub the ink off before it dries and it will just stay in the cracks.

12. Add another coat of varnish and your masterpiece is complete.

The Expert Says...

"If the pinnacle of Western art is arguably Leonardo da Vinci, his shadow self in the pantheon of forgers is Han van Meegeren."

— Frank Wynne, author of *I Was Vermeer*

pinnacle: *highest point*
pantheon: *group of persons most highly regarded for contributions to a field or endeavor*

Quick Fact

So that he wouldn't get caught, van Meegeren had to keep everything that he was doing secret. He couldn't even hire models to sit for his paintings because he was scared that they might tell his secret.

Take Note

Van Meegeren is #2 for good reasons: he fooled Abraham Bredius, a leading art expert; he tricked Nazi Hermann Goering; and he avoided the death sentence by proving he was a great forger — right in court.

• Although he only made a dozen forgeries, van Meegeren earned the equivalent of millions of dollars over the course of his career. Think about this: Is it more amazing for a forger to paint lots of fakes, or to make lots of money and fool important art critics with just a few fakes?

5 4

2

1

It was clear that Zhang Daqian wanted to make an impression. Although he lived during modern times, he dressed in robes and carried a large wooden staff. He also grew a long wispy beard in the ancient style.

IDENTITY: (1899–1983) Zhang Daqian (Chang Dai-chien) was one of China's most famous artists.

GREAT FAKES: Zhang was a busy guy! He completed about 30,000 paintings during his lifetime. His fakes span 1,000 years of Chinese art.

Like the script for a TV show, Zhang's life story is filled with excitement, strange events, and unusual people! As a young man, Zhang was kidnapped by bandits, joined a Buddhist monastery, and spent almost three years copying paintings in the mysterious Caves of the Thousand Buddhas in China.

In 1949, Zhang smuggled a huge collection of scrolls and paintings out of China. He later sold them illegally. Zhang was friends with gangsters and lived all over the world. He lived for 20 years on his $5 million, 35-acre Brazilian estate. The estate had a lake, a forest, monkeys, tigers, and bears. He lived with many wives (at the same time!), dozens of children, and still had time to paint approximately 30,000 original and forged paintings over the course of his life! Zhang is known for his silk work, his Chinese calligraphy, and his flawless painting technique. His forgeries are so good that many museums have had to defend their so-called authentic works against accusations that they may in fact be fakes by Zhang.

ZHANG DAQIAN

BUT WHY?

Zhang Daqian started copying famous paintings both to study them and for the challenge. It was a thrill to trick the important people in Shanghai. Later his reasons became financial. As he told a friend, "I need millions to support my family."

AND HOW?

In China, art owners signed and stamped their names onto their paintings. Each time the art changed hands, the new owner added his or her stamp to the work. Zhang used fake royal stamps (that he made) on his forgeries to make it look as if his works had been signed by emperors hundreds of years earlier. He also mastered and forged hundreds of signatures. He used very old brushes, ink, and antique silks to trick experts about the age of his paintings.

Quick Fact

A work by Zhang entitled *Crimson Lotuses on Gold Screen* recently sold for approximately $2.9 million at an auction house in Hong Kong! This was a new auction record for modern Chinese paintings.

EXPOSED!

While he has been exposed as a forger, Zhang was never actually caught during his lifetime. More than 20 years after his death, historians and experts are busy trying to find out how many "historical" Chinese paintings are actually the work of Zhang Daqian.

AS A RESULT ...

Because Zhang copied so many paintings, Chinese art collectors can't tell which pieces are real and which are fake. Even today, no one can be 100 percent sure that any collection of Chinese art is completely original.

Quick Fact

To create 30,000 paintings, Zhang Daqian would have had to paint two paintings per day for 40 years!

10   9   8   7   6

MASTER & FORGER

Zhang's forgeries of Chinese masterpieces earned him a place of honor in the art forging world. This article looks at the talent and skill required for Zhang to perfect his crime.

In his later years, Zhang's failing eyesight made him shift to a new style, in which large splashes of dark ink and color are made into mysterious and emotional images.

Zhang mastered an unbelievable 100 styles of painting and calligraphy. He also created his own magnificent paintings.

Zhang did everything! He gathered the antique silk on which to paint, he researched his subjects, and he painted the forgeries. The key to Zhang's success, aside from the convincing beauty of his paintings, was the realistic history of ownership that he created for his pictures. In Western art, the origin of a painting is usually described in a series of letters, catalogs, or stories. In Chinese art, the history of a work is seen right on the piece. In China, it was the tradition for every owner of a painting to stamp it with a seal as it was handed down or sold. So, as well as forging the painting, Zhang had to master each different type of signature. He then had to select from among the 970 seals he had in his possession (it is believed these were forged too) to show all of the owners through time. The number of paintings forged, and the difficulty of the paintings Zhang copied, is simply amazing.

Zhang Daqian, who died in 1983, is the most mysterious, most productive, and perhaps the most eccentric forger in history!

? It is up to scientists and art historians to test the paint and canvas and to study the painting to see if it is genuine. Why is it so hard to tell if a painting is real or fake?

The Expert Says…

" For Zhang, copying paintings was not a crime. He would say, 'The person who wants to buy it is the guilty one … I am not a forger, I improved it actually.' "

— William Kiang, former Chinese diplomat

? What does this quote tell you about Zhang's personality?

Take Note

At #1, Zhang Daqian is in a league all his own. He produced more fake paintings than most forgers, but he was never caught. That fact alone should set him up as the #1 forger of all time!
• What makes a forger "successful" — that he or she was never caught or the quality or the quantity of the fakes?

5   4   3   2   **1**

We Thought …

Here are the criteria we used in ranking the 10 most successful art forgers.

The forger:
- Was successful in damaging the confidence of buyers
- Had a global impact on the art world
- Created a large number of forged paintings
- Was able to forge paintings in a wide variety of styles
- Was able to fool experienced art critics
- Was able to mastermind complicated forging scams
- Had the ability to use his criminal background to find fame and fortune
- Was able to create believable fake documents and provenances
- Was able to create works of art that were as beautiful as those of famous artists

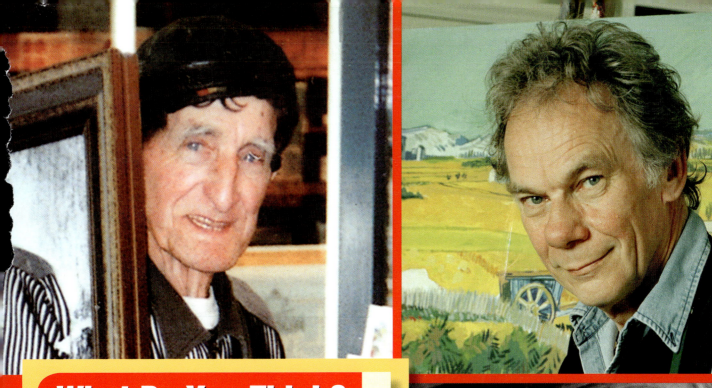

What Do You Think?

1. Do you agree with our ranking? If you don't, try ranking them yourself. Justify your ranking with data from your own research and reasoning. You may refer to our criteria, or you may want to draw up your own list of criteria.

2. Here are three other forgers that we considered but in the end did not include in our top 10 list: Claude-Émile Schuffenecker, David Stein, and Alceo Dossena.
   - Find out more about them. Do you think they should have made our list? Give reasons for your response.
   - Are there other art forgers who you think should have made our list? Explain your choices.

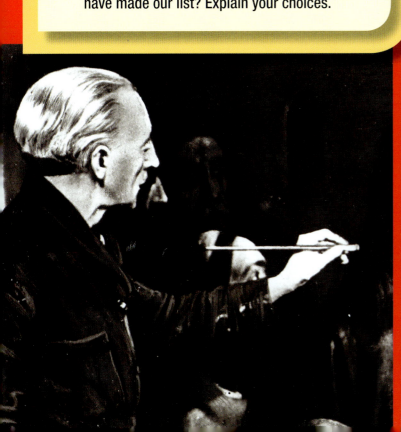

47

Index